3\09

BRAIN CANCER

**Current and Emerging Trends
in Detection and Treatment**

JERI FREEDMAN

ROSEN
PUBLISHING®

New York

Published in 2009 by The Rosen Publishing Group, Inc.
29 East 21st Street, New York, NY 10010

Library of Congress Cataloging-in-Publication Data

Freedman, Jeri.
Brain cancer: current and emerging trends in detection and treatment / Jeri Freedman.—1st ed.
    p. cm.—(Cancer and modern science)
Includes bibliographical references and index.
ISBN-13: 978-1-4358-5011-8 (library binding)
1. Brain—Cancer—Popular works. I. Title.
RC280.B7F74 2008
616.99'481—dc22

                                                    2008022086

Manufactured in the United States of America

On the cover: A computer-generated image of a tumor (yellow) growing on a neuron (pink) in the brain.

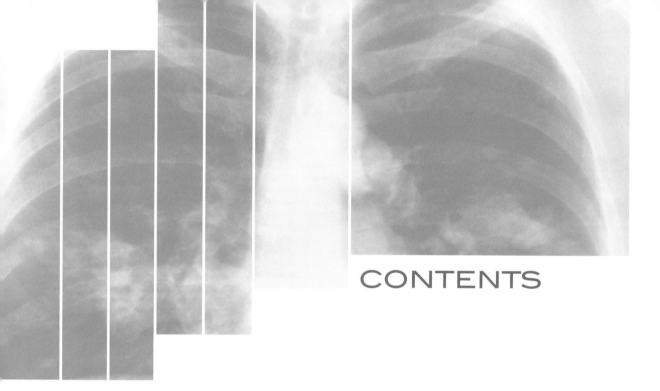

CONTENTS

INTRODUCTION

In the body, cells constantly mature and die, and new cells are created. The growth of cells is controlled by genes. When cancer occurs, a group of cells reproduces and grows out of control because the gene that normally regulates the rate of cell growth is defective.

When a brain tumor occurs, the ever-growing mass of cells compresses and damages other cells in the brain, interfering with brain function. The tumor pushes brain tissue around, creates pressure by pressing against the bones of the skull, and infiltrates (or invades) healthy brain tissue and the areas around the nerves. As a result, the tumor damages the tissues in the brain.

There are more than 120 types of brain cancer. Unlike other forms of cancer, which are associated with lifestyle activities such as smoking, dietary factors, or drinking, there is little known about why primary brain cancer occurs. Most brain cancer is the result of genetic mutations or changes in the genes that normally keep cells from reproducing in an uncontrolled manner.

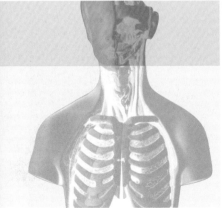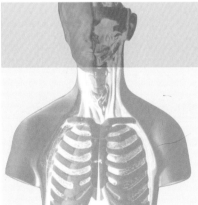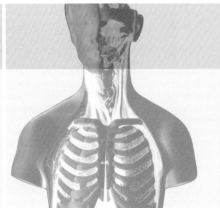

The 11th Annual Cassidy and Pinkard Colliers Race for Hope was held in Washington, D.C., in May 2008. This annual event is one of the largest national fund-raisers to benefit the brain tumor community.

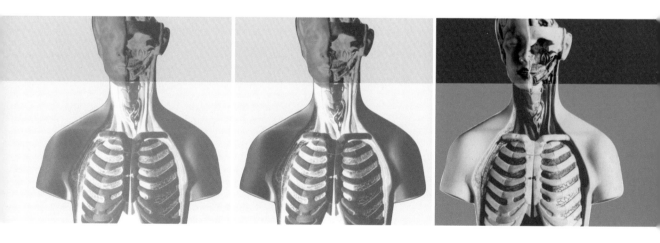

In the United States, between fifteen and twenty people out of every one hundred thousand develop brain cancer every year. It is the most common type of cancer that causes death in people under the age of thirty-five. Because brain cancer is not associated with lifestyle or environmental factors that most people encounter, there is no known way to guard against it at this time. But genetic research and gene-based treatments offer great hope for a breakthrough and a possible cure for this dreaded disease.

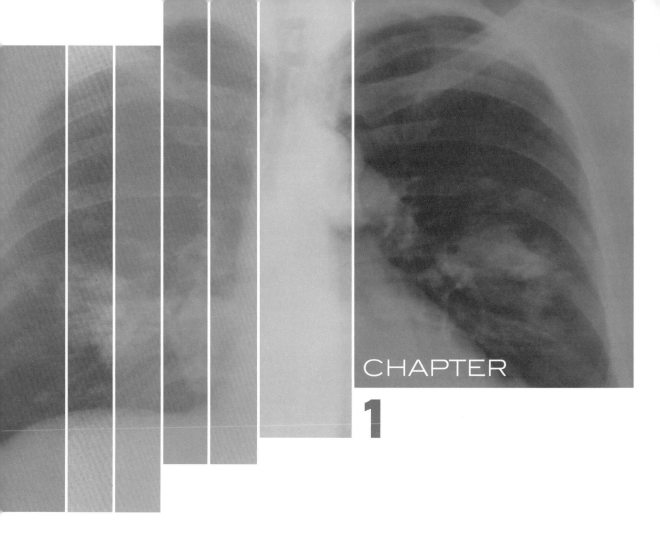

CHAPTER

1

TYPES OF BRAIN CANCER AND BRAIN TUMORS

Different parts of the brain control different physical and mental functions. The biggest area of the brain is the cerebrum. It consists of two halves, or hemispheres, connected by a series of nerves. The left hemisphere of the brain controls the right side of the body, and the right hemisphere of the brain controls the left side of the body. Each hemisphere is further divided into four sections called lobes:

— **Frontal lobes:** Located at the front of the brain, they control reasoning, judgment, inhibition, mood, attention, some body

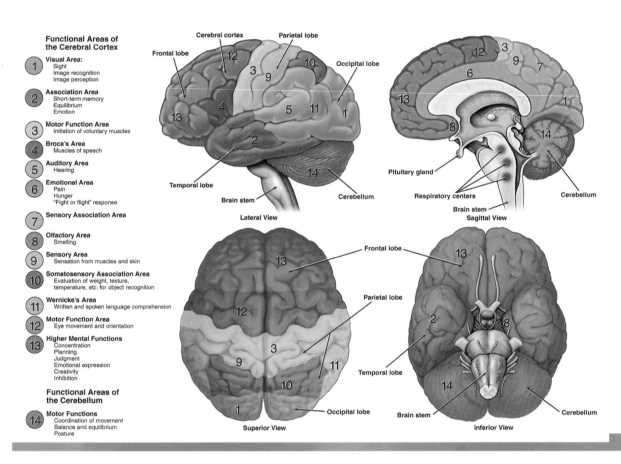

Functional Areas of the Cerebral Cortex

1 **Visual Area:**
Sight
Image recognition
Image perception

2 **Association Area**
Short-term memory
Equilibrium
Emotion

3 **Motor Function Area**
Initiation of voluntary muscles

4 **Broca's Area**
Muscles of speech

5 **Auditory Area**
Hearing

6 **Emotional Area**
Pain
Hunger
"Fight or flight" response

7 **Sensory Association Area**

8 **Olfactory Area**
Smelling

9 **Sensory Area**
Sensation from muscles and skin

10 **Somatosensory Association Area**
Evaluation of weight, texture, temperature, etc. for object recognition

11 **Wernicke's Area**
Written and spoken language comprehension

12 **Motor Function Area**
Eye movement and orientation

13 **Higher Mental Functions**
Concentration
Planning
Judgment
Emotional expression
Creativity
Inhibition

Functional Areas of the Cerebellum

14 **Motor Functions**
Coordination of movement
Balance and equilibrium
Posture

Cerebral cortex — Parietal lobe — Frontal lobe — Occipital lobe — Temporal lobe — Brain stem — Cerebellum — **Lateral View**

Pituitary gland — Respiratory centers — Brain stem — Cerebellum — **Sagittal View**

Frontal lobe — Parietal lobe — Temporal lobe — Occipital lobe — **Superior View**

Brain stem — Cerebellum — **Inferior View**

This diagram shows four different views of the human brain. Each image is color-coded to highlight the brain's anatomy and functional areas. A key at left explains the color code.

movement, and bowel and bladder control. Damage to the frontal lobes can affect one's sense of consequences and notions of good and bad, resulting in reckless or rule-breaking behavior. **Temporal lobes:** Located in the lower part of the cerebrum, they control hearing-related activity and long-term memory. In most people, the left temporal lobe is responsible for understanding language. In about 5 percent of people, the language function is located in the right temporal lobe.

— **Parietal lobes:** Located in the upper center of the cerebrum, they process sensory information and spatial orientation. They also play a role in reading, writing, and performing mathematical calculations.

— **Occipital lobes:** Located at the back of the cerebrum, they control vision. The right occipital lobe processes information from the left eye, while the left occipital lobe processes information from the right eye.

Below the cerebrum is the brain stem, which is divided into three parts: the midbrain, which is closest to the cerebrum; the pons; and the medulla oblongata. Information related to sight, hearing, smell, movement, and balance is transmitted from nerves through the spinal cord to the brain stem via twelve cranial nerves. The areas that control sleeping and waking and involuntary body functions—those we don't control consciously, such as the beating of the heart—are also located in the brain stem. The brain contains two major types of cells: nerve cells, which send and receive electrical signals; and glial cells, which provide the supporting and protective structure for nerve cells.

PRIMARY AND SECONDARY BRAIN TUMORS

Depending on where a brain tumor is located, it will affect different aspects of movement, senses, and behavior. There are a large variety of tumors. They originate in various parts of the brain and grow from different types of cells. Some types of brain cancer are seen more often in adults, while others are more frequent in children. Most occur equally in men and women, but some are more common in one gender than the other.

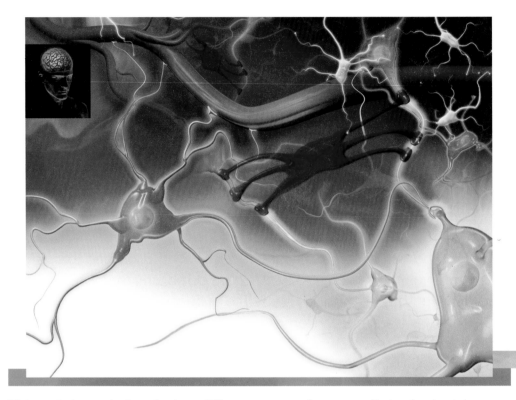

This artist's rendering depicts different types of nerve cells in the brain's grey matter, a collection of nerve cells that is a major component of the body's central nervous system.

Brain cancer is divided into two categories: primary brain cancer and metastatic brain cancer. Primary brain cancer is cancer that results from an abnormal growth of cells that starts in the brain itself. In the United States, about nineteen thousand people are diagnosed with primary brain cancer annually. Primary brain tumors are divided into groups: glial tumors and nonglial tumors. Glial tumors grow from cells in the fibers that support the nerve cells in the brain. Nonglial tumors grow from the nerves, glands, or blood vessels in the brain.

Secondary brain cancer, also called metastatic brain cancer, comes from cancer that starts in another body organ, such as the breast, colon, lung, or liver. The cancer metastasizes, or spreads, from the original site to other areas of the body, such as the brain. Cancerous cells from another part of the body travel through the blood to the brain. Once there, it starts reproducing in the same out-of-control way as the cells in the original tumor. Once cancer has metastasized, the patient has a smaller chance of survival than if the cancer is caught before it spreads. About half of all brain cancer is primary and half is the result of cancer that has metastasized from some other part of the body.

BENIGN VS. MALIGNANT TUMORS

There are two types of primary brain tumors: benign and malignant. A benign tumor is a cluster of cells that builds up in the brain. It usually grows slowly and does not invade nearby tissue or spread to other parts of the body. Such a tumor may present serious problems if it affects nearby brain tissue, causing symptoms such as loss of sight or hearing. It may become life threatening if it affects critical structures in the brain, such as major blood vessels.

Malignant tumors are fast growing and aggressively invade nearby tissue. Malignant tumors

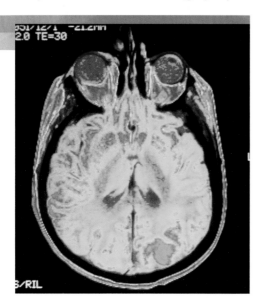

This MRI image shows a human brain. The bright blue spots indicate that cancer has metastasized (or spread) throughout the occipital lobe.

are always life threatening because there is a high likelihood that they will invade and damage tissue in the brain. Although no one knows why, sometimes benign tumors, if left untreated for a long period of time, will change into malignant tumors.

The brain and the spinal cord together make up the central nervous system, which sends signals to and receives them from all parts of the body. Primary brain tumors that are malignant can spread from the brain to the spinal cord. However, unlike many other forms of cancer, it is rare for tumors that start in the brain to metastasize and spread to other parts of the body.

COMMON BRAIN TUMORS

There are more than 120 types of brain tumors. The following are some of the most common.

COMMON GLIAL TUMORS

The most common type of glial tumor is called an astrocytoma (*astro* is Latin for "star," and *cyto* means "cell"). This type of tumor grows from glial cells that are called astrocytes because they are star-shaped. This type of tumor can occur in almost any part of the brain. In children, this type of tumor usually grows slowly, but in adults, it can be very aggressive. In adults, astrocytomas are more likely to affect the spinal cord.

The nerve cells of the brain are surrounded by an insulating sheath of a fatty material called myelin. There is a type of tumor called an oligodendroglioma, which grows from the cells of this myelin sheath. This type of tumor primarily affects young to middle-aged adults. Frequently, brain tumors are found to be a combination of oligodendrogliomas and astrocytomas.

Another type of glial tumor is the ependymoma. The brain has ventricles that are butterfly-shaped openings in the center of the brain through which spinal fluid flows around the central nervous system.

The red structures in this rendering are astrocyte cells that regulate the nerve signals of the neuron (yellow). The most common type of glial brain tumors, astrocytomas, occur in astrocyte cells.

Ependymomas grow from the cells that line these ventricles and the spinal cord. About 10 percent of brain tumors in children are ependymomas.

COMMON NONGLIAL TUMORS

Lymphoma is a type of cancer that grows from lymphocytes, or white blood cells. These are immune system cells that normally travel through the body fighting infection. In the central nervous system, these cells grow out of control, forming tumors in the brain and sometimes in the spinal cord as well.

Chordomas usually occur in adults who are in their twenties and thirties. They are slow-growing tumors that can metastasize. They grow from leftover bits of the pre-spinal-cord structure that is replaced by the spinal cord as a fetus develops.

Medulloblastoma is an aggressive, malignant tumor that occurs most commonly in the cerebellum, the part of the brain above and behind the brain stem, at the back of the head. Although this type of tumor

The circular structures in this microscopic photograph are myelin sheaths that are wrapped around nerve fibers. A type of brain tumor known as an oligodendroglioma can grow in the cells of these sheaths.

does appear in adults, it's more common in children. About 25 percent of tumors are medulloblastomas. They affect boys more than girls.

BENIGN TUMORS

Several types of benign tumors form in the brain or within the cranial area. Though not malignant or life threatening, they can cause serious health problems.

About 10 percent of tumors grow from cells of the pituitary gland, a gland in the brain that releases hormones, or substances that regulate growth and body functions. This type of tumor is called an adenoma and is usually benign. It is rare in children and occurs primarily in adolescents and adults. The pituitary gland is found inside the skull, just above the nasal passages. It is considered the master control gland of hormone production because it regulates the activity of most other glands in the body. It has a particularly important role in adolescence as it regulates the hormones that begin to be produced at the onset of puberty, triggering all of the physical changes that usher teens into adulthood.

Adenomas usually do not spread beyond the area of the pituitary, and though benign, they can cause serious health problems. Because the space is so tight in that part of the skull, even a small growth can create crowding that results in vision problems and hormone deficiencies (when the tumor constricts pituitary tissue). Larger adenomas, called macroadenomas, even release their own pituitary hormones, which can result in hormone overproduction and related growth, metabolism, menstruation, ovulation, and sperm-production problems.

Tumors found in the skull or in the spinal column are among the few benign tumors that require aggressive treatment and removal because of the sensitivity of their location in the central nervous system. Benign tumors can place pressure on sensitive nerve and brain tissues, and they can harm the normal functioning of the nervous system and brain. For example, meningiomas are tumors that originate in the outer covering of the brain but may spread to the skull or spinal column. (About 27 percent of all primary brain tumors are meningiomas.) Some meningiomas grow near the optic nerve, squeezing it and causing vision loss.

Orbital tumors are tumors that occur in the eye socket, eyeball, eye muscles, and optical nerve. Several different kinds of benign tumors can form in these locations, including dermoids (cysts of the lining of bone), lymphangiomas and hemangiomas (blood vessel tumors), and lyorbital cellulites (infections that usually starts as a severe sinus infection and spread to the orbital area). Cancerous tumors can also occur in the orbital area. Presence of a tumor, whether benign or cancerous, is usually signaled by a "prominent" or swollen eye, pain, redness, and blurred or double vision. While some benign orbital tumors require no treatment, others that impinge on the optic nerve or otherwise affect vision may require surgery or radiation.

In Latin, the name of the condition known as pseudotumor cerebri literally means "false brain tumor," and that is exactly what it is. It is not a tumor at all but a buildup of fluid in the brain. The fluid buildup creates pressure and results in symptoms typically associated with brain tumors, including headaches, nausea, and vision problems. Treatment is fairly straightforward and usually nonsurgical. Most of the time, drugs are prescribed that help drain excess fluid from the brain.

Tuberous sclerosis is a neurological disorder that creates serious symptoms, such as seizures, mental retardation, and skin lesions. The condition is also characterized by the growth of benign tumors in the brain, kidneys, heart, and lungs. To date, there is no cure for the condition, but the symptoms can be treated.

A benign tumor found deep inside the brain is especially dangerous because surgery to remove it may damage vital brain centers. In such cases, radiation may be used to shrink the tumor. A benign tumor located closer to the brain's surface can usually be removed surgically with minimal risk and complications. The main symptoms of brain tumors include headaches, seizures, nausea and vomiting, hearing and vision problems, coordination and balance problems (including muscle weakness), and even personality changes and decreased mental abilities (such as speech, thinking, and memory). Symptoms of spinal cord tumors include pain, muscle weakness, loss of feeling or sensation, and motor skill problems.

RISK FACTORS AND PREVENTION

Unlike other forms of cancer, which are often associated with lifestyle activities such as smoking, dietary factors, or drinking, there is little known about why primary brain cancer occurs. Researchers are investigating a number of potential causes, including the possible involvement of viruses, chemicals, and genetic factors.

Brain cancer is definitely associated with one environmental factor: exposure to vinyl chloride, a chemical used in making plastics. If one lives near a plant that uses vinyl chloride or a toxic waste site where this material may have been disposed of then there is a chance that this material may have leaked into the local water supply. However, in most cases of brain tumors, there has not been exposure to this chemical.

Most brain cancer is the result of genetic mutations or changes in the genes that normally keep cells from reproducing in an uncontrolled manner. These genes are called tumor suppressor genes. When one of these genes is altered or deleted, the brake on cell growth is removed, and tumors can form. Some forms of brain cancer are known to be inherited. However, brain tumors sometimes occur in people with no family history of such tumors. This may be the result of a spontaneous mutation that occurred in the genetic material carried in the egg or sperm cells, or from factors that researchers have not yet identified.

Since brain cancer is not associated with specific lifestyle choices (such as cigarette smoking or alcohol consumption) or environmental factors that most people encounter, there is no known way to guard against it at this time. The symptoms that a person who has brain cancer experiences depend on the type of brain cancer he or she has. Symptoms also depend on the location of the tumor because different areas of the brain control different functions.

MYTHS AND FACTS

MYTH   You can get brain cancer from using a cell phone.

FACT   Controlled studies have not shown a relationship between cancer and cell phone use. Given the number of teenagers with cell phones and the amount of time they spend on them, there would be a much higher rate of cancer among teens than there is.

MYTH   More people are dying of cancer every year.

FACT   More people are being diagnosed with cancer because: (1) the population of the United States is aging, and as people age, their chances of getting cancer is greater; and (2) our detection methods have gotten better, so more cases are being caught. In fact, more people are surviving cancer than ever before because the cancer is being caught earlier and treatments have improved.

MYTH   A head injury can result in brain tumors.

FACT   Injuries don't cause cancer. In the course of administering a brain scan following a head injury, a doctor may coincidentally detect a tumor, but the tumor was not caused by the head injury. Blows to the head can cause other types of problems, however, such as bleeding into the brain. So, if you lose consciousness, get a headache, have blurry vision, or have other symptoms after an injury, see a doctor immediately.

MYTH Keeping an upbeat attitude, meditating, or praying will cure cancer.

FACT Only proper medical treatment will cure cancer. However, there is some evidence that people with a good mental attitude recover better and cope better with their illness. This may be because these approaches reduce stress, which adversely affects the body, and because such people are more hopeful and confident, and, therefore, more active in attempting to improve their condition. It is important to emphasize, though, that cancer cannot be cured by any mental or spiritual approach alone. Medical treatment is still necessary.

MYTH Alternative health techniques can cure cancer.

FACT Alternative health techniques, such as acupuncture, massage, or herbal supplements, can help treat some symptoms resulting from cancer treatment, like pain, nausea, or emotional stress. By themselves, however, these alternative techniques will not make a tumor go away. Conventional treatment is still required.

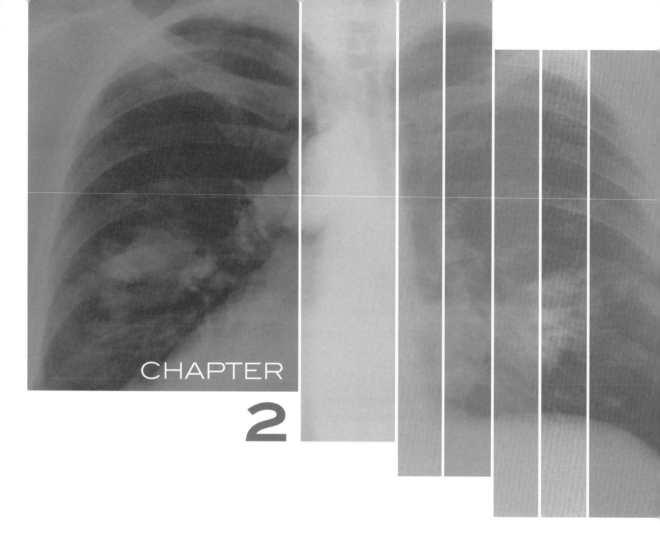

CHAPTER 2

DETECTION AND DIAGNOSIS

Brain cancer diagnosis starts with a discussion between the patient and a doctor about the symptoms the patient is experiencing. If the symptoms indicate the possibility of a brain tumor, then the patient will be given a neurological examination and possibly a brain scan. In some cases, a biopsy is performed.

SYMPTOMS OF BRAIN TUMORS

Since different parts of the brain control different body functions and behaviors, brain tumors can produce many different types of symptoms.

Some of these symptoms may be specific to certain locations—for example, affecting sight, hearing, or balance. Other symptoms are more general. Symptoms commonly experienced by people suffering from brain tumors include:

- **Headaches:** Many people with a brain tumor experience headaches, which may last from several minutes to hours. The headaches may become worse if the person alters his or her position or coughs. However, headaches can have many causes, so this alone is not enough to indicate a brain tumor.
- **Vomiting:** Pressure inside the skull can result in nausea and vomiting, sometimes along with a headache.
- **Vision or hearing difficulties:** Vision and hearing problems can result from three causes: (1) Increased pressure in the skull can lead to swelling of the optic nerve and double or blurred vision or partial loss of vision. (2) Tumors can grow in the occipital lobe region, where visual information is processed, resulting in apparent vision loss. (3) Tumors growing around or from sensory nerves can result in abnormal eye movement, crossed eyes, loss of

Frequent and persistent headaches are a classic symptom of brain tumors, though headaches can have many other less-threatening causes, too.

vision, loss of hearing, or hearing strange sounds, such as ringing or buzzing.

— **Movement problems:** Sometimes, tumors affect areas of the brain that control movement. In that case, a person may have problems with weakness or paralysis and may experience difficulty with walking and coordination. If an area that controls balance is affected, then a person may experience dizziness and/or have trouble maintaining balance.

— **Emotional or behavioral problems:** When a tumor is located in the parts of the brain that control reasoning, judgment, impulse control, communication, or emotion, the person may experience changes in behavior and emotional response. For example, an ordinarily quiet person may suddenly seem angry and aggressive. A normally controlled person may suddenly become extremely impulsive. Or a typically intelligent and articulate person may suddenly develop problems in understanding or communicating. When the area of the brain responsible for memory is affected, a person will experience memory problems.

— **Seizures:** Nerve cells communicate with each other by sending and receiving electrical signals. When the electrical activity in the brain becomes disordered, as sometimes occurs with a brain tumor, it is called a seizure. Seizures result in a variety of symptoms ranging from unconsciousness to convulsions (involuntary contractions of the muscles that cause violent movements of the body).

THE NEUROLOGICAL EVALUATION

In a neurological examination, the doctor tests the patient's physical reflexes, strength, muscle control, balance, and other physical factors. This may involve having the patient perform various physical actions to evaluate strength, muscle control, and coordination. A doctor may test the patient's reflexes by tapping joints like the knees with a tiny hammer. Sensory testing may also be conducted by touching parts of the arms or legs with a device that produces a pricking sensation. The doctor also tests the patient's mental responses. If the physical and/or mental responses are not within the normal range, then the doctor may either order a brain scan or refer the patient to a doctor who specializes in treating diseases of the central nervous system. There are two types of specialists who treat diseases of the central nervous system. Neurologists treat diseases of the brain and spinal cord. Neurosurgeons perform surgery on the brain and spinal cord.

IMAGING THE BRAIN

There are several different types of brain scans that can be used to produce pictures

Testing reflexes, muscle strength and control, and coordination are important first steps in diagnosing possible brain tumors.

of the brain. Brain scans use computer technology to create these pictures. These pictures allow doctors to see all the structures in the brain, including any abnormal ones. There are three main types of scans: magnetic resonance imaging (MRI), computed tomography (CT or CAT scans), and positron electron imaging (PET).

MAGNETIC RESONANCE IMAGING (MRI)

In an MRI, the patient is placed in a tube-like chamber. Inside the machine are large electromagnets that surround the platform on which the patient lies. When they are turned on, the electromagnets

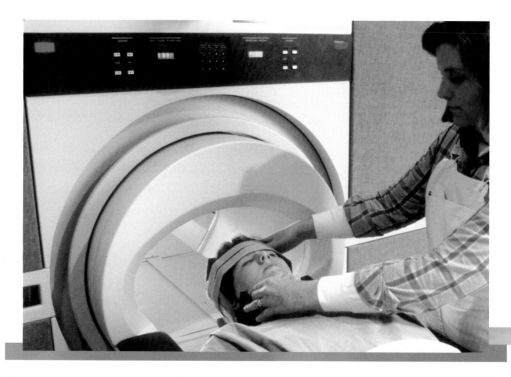

A patient is being prepared to undergo an MRI exam. The machine's powerful electromagnets will produce a detailed image of the patient's brain, allowing for a more accurate diagnosis.

create a magnetic field. When this field interacts with the patient's tissue, it produces data that the computer can analyze to produce a detailed picture of the inside of the body part being imaged—in this case, the brain. Because MRIs do not use X-ray technology, they do not expose the patient to radiation. However, because they use magnetic fields, they can interact with pacemakers and metal implants, such as pins or plates used to repair broken bones. So, you should tell the doctor or imaging technician if you have any of these. MRIs take a series of pictures, each of which is a thin slice of the brain. The computer then combines all of the sequential pictures to produce a three-dimensional image of the brain.

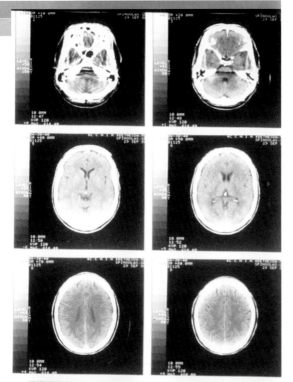

COMPUTED TOMOGRAPHY (CT) SCANS

CT scans use X-ray technology and computer analysis to provide pictures of tissues, blood vessels, and bones. In order to

Pictured here is a series of CT scans of a single brain. When CT scans were first introduced in the 1970s, they revolutionized the detection and diagnosis of brain tumors.

make the tissue stand out more, a dye is often injected into the patient. Since this dye may contain iodine, people allergic to iodine should let the doctor or imaging technician know. CT scans can show bleeding and swelling, as well as some tumors.

POSITRON ELECTRON (PET) SCANS

PET scans don't take a picture of the brain itself. Instead, they record electrical activity in the different parts of the brain. The brain uses a type of sugar called glucose as fuel. The PET scan is used to measure the activity in a tumor by seeing how much glucose it is absorbing. A type of glucose is combined with a weak radioactive marker and is injected into a patient. As the glucose is absorbed by the brain, the PET scan records the amount of radioactivity in specific areas, and this information is analyzed by a computer. PET scans are useful not only for identifying areas that contain tumor cells, but also for locating scar tissue and brain tissue that has been destroyed by treatment.

BIOPSY

In a biopsy, a small piece of tissue is removed from a tumor. This tissue is examined in a laboratory to gain information about the structure of the cells in the tumor. In most cases of suspected brain cancer, when a biopsy is performed, a piece of bone is removed from the skull. A neurosurgeon then removes all or part of the tumor, and the bone is usually put back.

When a tumor is located in an area that is difficult to reach, the doctor may instead perform a closed biopsy. In this case, the surgeon drills a small hole in the skull, inserts a hollow needle into the tumor, and removes a piece of the tissue. The tissue removed from the tumor is sent to a laboratory, where it is examined under a microscope to evaluate the tumor cells. The main reason for performing a biopsy is to be able to grade the tumor.

GRADING A TUMOR

Doctors grade tumors to indicate how advanced a given type of cancer is. This grading basically consists of describing the characteristics or changes seen in cells as cancer progresses.

A widely accepted system for grading tumors is the one established by the World Health Organization (WHO). A tumor is assigned a grade based on how similar the structure of its cells is to that of normal cells, how fast the cells are growing, and how likely they are to spread. The higher the grade, the more advanced the tumor is. For example, tumors that are self-contained (have not grown into surrounding tissue) and are slow-growing are often called grade I (and are considered benign or mildly malignant). Malignant tumors, which have grown into surrounding tissue, are categorized according to how advanced they are as grade II, III, or IV. Sometimes, such tumors are also referred to using the terms "low grade," "mid-grade," and "high grade," depending on their severity.

After a biopsy sample is taken, a pathologist (a doctor who specializes in analyzing diseases) examines it under a microscope and indicates whether the tumor is benign or malignant, what type of cells are involved in the tumor, and what the grade of the tumor is. This information provides the doctor with information that will help in establishing the most appropriate treatment.

TEN GREAT QUESTIONS
TO ASK YOUR DOCTOR

1. What changes in mood, behavior, or physical or mental abilities might I experience as the result of brain cancer or its treatment?

2. What are the signs that the cancer might be getting worse?

3. Are there medications I can take that would help with the symptoms?

4. What activities are OK for me to engage in?

5. What should I do if I experience problems in class?

6. Are there support groups that I can join for this problem?

7. How often should I have a checkup?

8. Would seeing a physical or occupational therapist help me with disabilities caused by the cancer?

9. Are there special devices that would help me compensate for the disabilities I might experience?

10. Would you write me a note explaining the nature of my disease to my teachers?

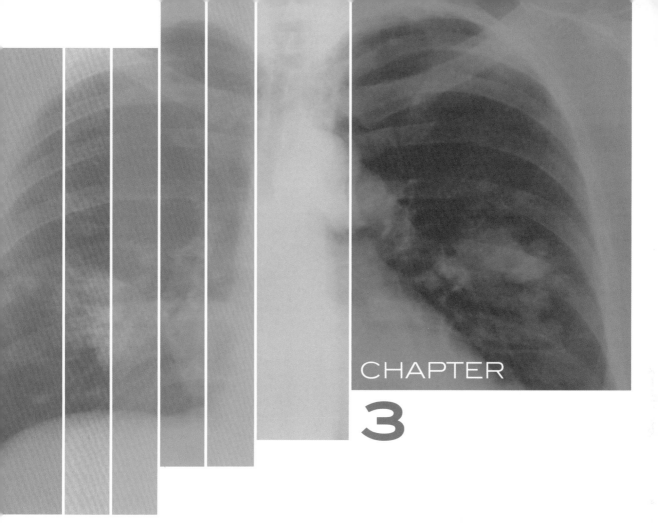

TREATMENT

Most tumors are treated by one or more of the following techniques: surgery, chemotherapy, and/or radiation. In most cases, the treatment of a brain tumor is handled by a team of doctors and other specialists. These experts frequently include a neurosurgeon, a neurologist, and an oncologist (a doctor who specializes in the treatment of cancer).

SURGERY

Surgery is the primary technique used to treat tumors whenever possible. This type of surgery performed on the brain is called a

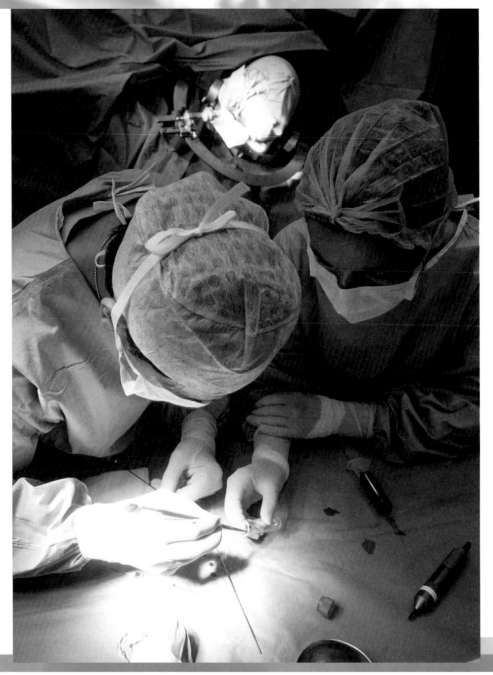

A surgeon and an assistant perform a biopsy. The tissue samples they extract will be analyzed to see if any of the cells are cancerous.

craniotomy. Prior to surgery, a patient may be given medications, such as steroids, to reduce swelling and inflammation. The neurosurgeon will attempt to remove the tumor, a process called resectioning. The goal is to do so while causing minimal disturbance to the surrounding structures.

A common surgical technique used in removing tumors is micro-surgery. In this type of surgery, the doctor looks through a mounted high-powered microscope. This device makes the tumor and surrounding tissue look much larger than they would with the naked eye. As a result, it is easier for the doctor to separate the tumor from the surrounding tissue and remove it. It is best to remove the entire tumor if possible because if it is not completely removed, it could regrow. Sometimes, because of its location, it is not possible to remove the entire tumor without causing significant damage to the surrounding tissue. In this case, as much of the tumor is removed as possible in order to reduce the symptoms it is causing. Then, the patient is treated with chemotherapy and/or radiation in an attempt to kill any cancer cells in the remaining section of tumor.

RADIATION THERAPY

In radiation therapy, high-energy X-rays or other types of radiation are applied to a tumor to kill the cancer cells. This approach is often used when a tumor is located in a place that makes surgery impossible, or when a tumor can only be partially removed.

Radiation therapy can be external or internal. In internal radiation therapy, pellets of radioactive material are implanted directly into the tumor, where the radiation will kill the surrounding cells. Internal radiation therapy is most often used for tumors that are small and hard to remove.

When radiation is applied externally, a machine is used to focus a high-energy X-ray beam on the area to be treated. In conventional radiation therapy, a patient receives a number of treatments given over a series of weeks and using small amounts of radiation. When the tumor is located in one specific area of the brain, focused radiation treatments are used. In this case, a machine is used that delivers a focused energy beam aimed directly at the specific site of the tumor. If the patient has multiple tumors or metastasized tumors, then another type of radiation therapy, called whole brain radiation therapy, is used. In this case, a wide beam of radiation (WRBT) is focused on the entire brain.

An alternative to conventional external radiation therapy is stereotactic radiosurgery (SRS). It cannot be used in all cases, but if the size and location of the tumor are appropriate, this technique is the preferred one. First, an MRI or

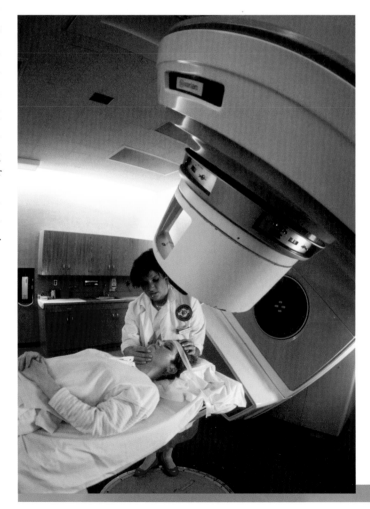

A patient is prepared to receive radiation therapy for cancer. She will receive externally applied radiation, with a beam focused upon the cancerous area by the machine above her.

CT scan is used to create a three-dimensional map of the area in which the tumor is located. This information allows a computer to precisely establish the location of the tumor. Doctors can use this technique to treat a tumor with a single high dose of radiation in one session, rather than multiple smaller doses over many weeks. And, if appropriate, a machine can be used to deliver a beam of radiation to the exact site of the tumor, often from multiple directions. Stereotactic imaging can also be used to better place radioactive pellets that will kill tumors with internal radiation therapy.

Short-term side effects of radiation therapy occur immediately after treatment. They include tiredness, nausea, loss of appetite, hair loss in the area being irradiated, and short-term memory loss. In most cases, the majority of these symptoms improve once the treatments are finished.

Sometimes, after they have been killed, the dead tumor cells re-form and become a new mass in the brain. Such a mass can cause the same type of symptoms as a tumor—memory loss, headaches, and personality or behavioral changes. The new mass may also

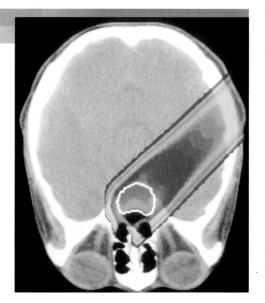

The red and yellow band in this CT scan is a proton beam zeroing in on a brain tumor (the pinkish red mass circled in white) during radiation therapy.

look like a tumor on a brain scan. Such masses are usually surgically removed or treated with steroids.

CHEMOTHERAPY

Conventional chemotherapy consists of a combination of medications that are taken orally or infused intravenously (directly into a vein). These medications kill fast-growing and dividing cells. Since cancer cells are constantly growing and dividing, the drugs help halt their rapid and uncontrolled growth. However, the medications may also affect other normally growing and dividing cells in the body, such as hair cells. This is why it is common for patients to lose their hair during chemotherapy.

Because the chemicals used in chemotherapy are so strong, they are usually given in a series of treatments at intervals. This allows the patient to rest and recover from the sometimes harsh effects of chemotherapy between treatments. Side effects of chemotherapy include hair loss, tiredness, chills, shortness of breath, nausea, and tingling in the patient's limbs.

POST-TREATMENT CHECKUPS

After treatment, it is important that patients continue to see their doctor at regular intervals to make sure that the tumor does not reoccur. When a tumor has been treated successfully and the cancer cells stop multiplying, the patient is said to be in remission. There is no way to tell if the tumor will or will not recur even after entering remission, so it is important to continue to see the doctor periodically. Most likely, a brain scan will be used to make sure that the tumor is not recurring.

COPING WITH DIAGNOSES AND TREATMENT

Dealing with the diagnosis of, treatment of, and recovery from brain cancer can be a scary and stressful experience. For this reason, you may

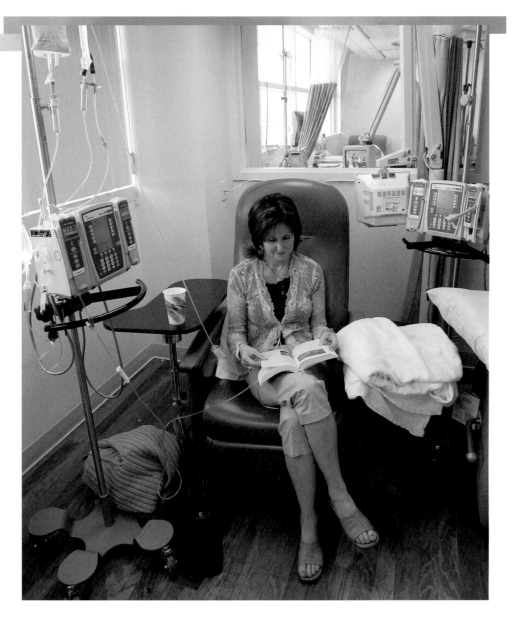

While receiving chemotherapy treatment, this patient tries to relax and read a book. The side effects of chemotherapy vary in kind and intensity from patient to patient.

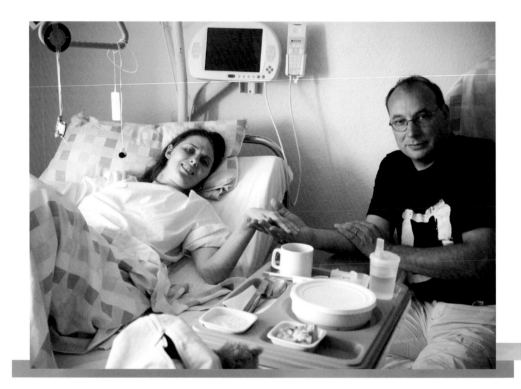

Both cancer victims and their families can be frightened and even traumatized by being diagnosed with and fighting the disease. It is important for them to get the help and support they need.

want to talk with a counselor who works with cancer patients and their families. In addition, there are a variety of support groups for people undergoing cancer treatment and for cancer survivors. A list of such groups can be found on the Web sites of reputable organizations such as the American Cancer Society (www.cancer.org) and the Brain Tumor Foundation (www.braintumor.org), as well as through recommendations at the facility where you obtain cancer treatment.

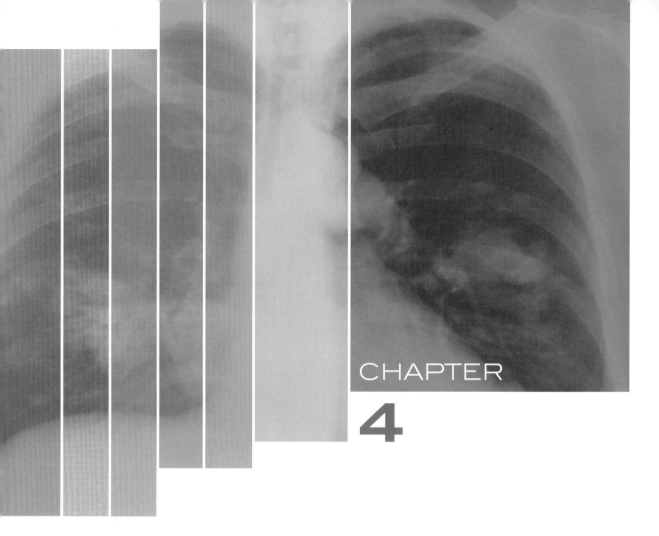

LIVING WITH BRAIN CANCER

There are both short-term and long-term issues that relate to living with brain cancer. Immediately after treatment, the patient may undergo rehabilitation to deal with the physical effects of removing the tumor and any side effects of treatment. Beyond this, there are issues that patients must deal with in the months and years following cancer treatment.

REHABILITATION AFTER TREATMENT

After treatment for brain cancer, you may experience problems in some areas as a result of both the cancer and the side effects of treatments

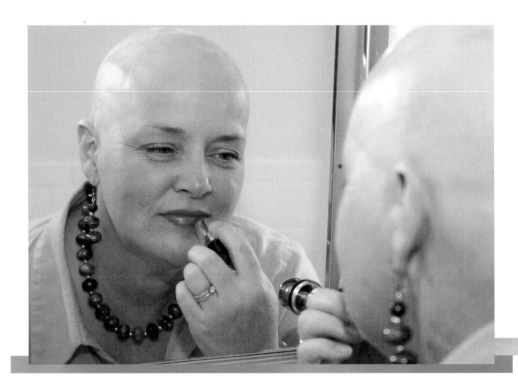

Losing one's hair is a common side effect of both radiation and chemotherapy, but it shouldn't stop anyone from getting out there and remaining active in life outside the home and hospital.

such as surgery. Depending on where the cancer was located, speech, movement, hearing, vision, or cognitive functions may be affected. If you have difficulties in any of these areas, then you will most likely be referred to one or more therapists for rehabilitation. This may involve working with specialists who treat particular problems. Some examples of experts in rehabilitation include physical, occupational, speech, and vision therapists. Physical therapists work with patients to improve movement and physical functioning. Occupational therapists help patients develop techniques to compensate for disabilities in their home and work environments. Speech therapists work with patients to improve their ability to speak. Vision therapists deal with patients' sight problems.

COGNITIVE REHABILITATION

If you experience problems with thinking, memory, emotional control, or other mental and personality-related problems, then this will often be addressed with cognitive rehabilitation. You may work with therapists who teach techniques for dealing with deficits such as memory loss. Vocational counselors can provide job training.

Brain cancer sometimes affects areas of the brain that control emotions or self-control. This can result in sudden mood swings or inappropriate behavior. Psychotherapists provide assistance with dealing with emotional problems—those that result from damage to the areas of the brain that affect emotion, and those relating to the traumatic experience of cancer diagnosis and treatment. Psychotherapists also play a key role at the beginning of rehabilitation by administering a standard set of tests for cognitive and emotional functioning. The results of these tests can be used by other therapists as a road map for administering appropriate therapy.

PHYSICAL THERAPY

It is not uncommon for someone with a brain tumor to have some physical effects after treatment. Common problems are weakness in one or more limbs, difficulty with balance, and tremors (shaking). If you experience such physical problems, then a physical therapist can provide exercises and other treatments designed to help you improve your physical abilities, such as strengthening weakened parts of the body or improving your balance and ability to walk.

Physical therapy may be necessary after treatment for brain cancer depending on where the tumor was growing and how it affected surrounding nerves and the related brain functions.

If your speech is affected, then a speech therapist can provide exercises to help you regain or improve your ability to speak. He or she can also teach you alternative ways of communicating if necessary. Speech therapists can help patients deal with difficulties related to swallowing food if these issues arise.

Some types of tumors affect a person's sight. This happens most commonly when tumors affect the visual cortex (the part of the brain responsible for processing sight), or when the tumor is located on the optic nerve, which runs from the back of the eye to the brain. If you experience a full or partial loss of sight, then a therapist can provide training in techniques that you can use to get around and function in the outside world. Following brain cancer, you may retain some vision but have trouble seeing. In this case, a vision therapist can provide information on and training in using devices such as special monitors that magnify items like book or newspaper pages.

EFFECTS ON GROWTH

Depending on the age when you develop brain cancer, you may or may not have reached your full growth. If the cancer occurs in the region of the pituitary gland, which produces hormones that regulate growth, then these hormones may no longer be produced after treatment. This could result in you not growing to a normal height. Therefore, it is important for your growth to be monitored. If you are a young teenager and do not appear to be growing normally, then it may be necessary to take injections of growth hormones to achieve normal growth.

COPING WITH SCHOOL AND COMMUNITY

In addition to actual cognitive problems resulting from a brain tumor, you may feel frustrated by the limitations resulting from your cancer when you return to school. If you experience physical issues with movement, hearing, or sight, then you may feel self-conscious and embarrassed. All of this can be very stressful, and the stress itself can make the situation worse. Be aware that there are special devices that you can use to assist you with seeing and hearing better in class. The rehabilitation therapists you will work with after your treatment can recommend which devices will be helpful to you and explain to you and your parents how to go about obtaining them and how to use them.

It's important for you and your parents to involve your teachers and other personnel at your school in arranging for special assistance in your classes. It is especially important to make your teachers aware of your capabilities as well as your limitations. For example, if your sight or hearing is limited but you are otherwise quite capable of learning in a normal academic program, then it is important for your teachers to understand this.

People are often uncomfortable with anything they are unfamiliar with or that is different from their usual experience. Therefore, it is possible that some of your classmates may avoid you or tease you. If you encounter difficulties with other students, then make sure you tell your parents and teachers about such problems so that they can deal with them. Don't assume, however, that your experiences with other students will necessarily be negative. Fellow classmates often turn out to be surprisingly helpful, supportive, and sympathetic, especially in a crisis or its aftermath.

GETTING BACK INTO THE SWING OF THINGS

There are a number of things that you can do to help yourself deal with your treatment and recovery. The first is to take care of yourself physically. Eat a healthy, well-balanced diet and get adequate rest and

exercise. This will help you stay in the best possible condition to cope with the physical demands of treatment and recovery and the effects of stress.

A healthy, well-balanced diet is a great preventative measure against all kinds of illnesses, including many types of cancer.

It is best to consider in advance the changes you may experience as a result of a tumor and its treatment. If you don't know what to expect, then ask questions of all the doctors and therapists you encounter. Then, prepare a strategy for coping with the limitations that you might confront. Be aware that not all of the side effects that you may experience may be permanent. Some conditions improve over time. As you go back to school and other activities, you may wish to work with a counselor or psychotherapist with whom you can discuss any anger or frustration you may experience. If you encounter difficulties from other students or teachers, then be sure to tell your parents right away so that they can take steps to deal with these problems.

An information specialist for the Cancer Information Service answers the questions of a concerned caller. Specialists like this can provide you with information, reassurance, and valuable coping strategies.

It is very important to have emotional support when coping with the effects of a brain tumor. There are many support groups for both patients and their families. These groups can provide vital emotional support and social interaction as well as practical advice. Information on local support groups, meeting places, and meeting times can be found in local newspapers and through local hospitals or health centers.

There are many things that you cannot control when you have a disease like brain cancer. However, it is important to participate in the activities in which you do have influence. You can develop strategies for coping with the obstacles you encounter and participate in as many decisions as you are able to. This fosters a sense of control and can help you cope. It is not easy to cope with all the life changes that a brain tumor may bring. However, it is important to stay involved with school and other community activities. Despite any limitations that you may encounter, remaining active and involved will allow you to continue to grow and develop as a person, maintain a positive outlook, and stay energized.

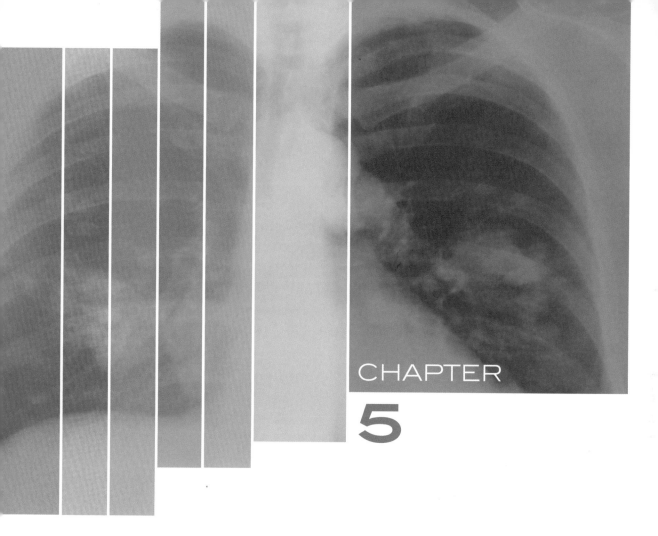

THE FUTURE TREATMENT OF BRAIN CANCER

Doctors are interested in developing new ways to treat brain tumors that are less invasive, are more effective, and produce fewer side effects. The following are some new approaches being explored in cancer treatment.

BETTER CHEMOTHERAPY

Today, the most commonly used combinations of chemotherapy drugs for treating brain cancer are carmustine, more often referred to by the initials BCNU, or lomustine, more commonly called CCNU. As mentioned earlier, chemotherapy drugs such as these have unpleasant side effects, including hair loss, tiredness, chills, shortness of breath, and nausea. Therefore, finding better chemotherapy drugs is a major area of research.

There are dozens of new combinations of chemicals being tested in the hope of developing better chemotherapy agents. One approach to finding new chemotherapy drugs is focused on developing drugs that would only affect the type of cell that composes the tumor. This would result in fewer side effects from the killing of other healthy cells during cancer treatment. Another approach is combining chemotherapy agents with other compounds to aid in their delivery. For instance, drugs combined with artificially produced forms of fat molecules called liposomes better penetrate the tumor cells. Cancer drugs that

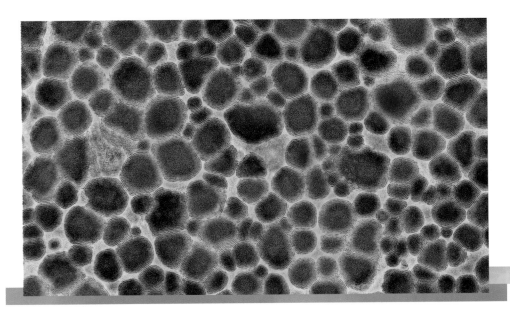

These artificially created liposome vesicles (fatty sacs) form a permeable membrane, or thin barrier, that can deliver toxic drugs to cancer cells in an attempt to kill them off.

piggyback on liposomes are more effective because they are delivered into the heart of the tumor. This approach is called liposomal therapy.

In treating brain tumors, doctors face an obstacle that they don't have to deal with when treating other types of cancer. This obstacle is the blood-brain barrier. It consists of an interlacing series of blood vessels and cells that filter blood entering the brain. This process removes potentially damaging substances from the blood before they can reach and affect the brain. Unfortunately, it also blocks compounds such as many chemotherapy drugs that could help treat brain cancer. Researchers are working to find drugs that would make this barrier permeable to chemotherapy agents that cannot presently cross it.

One new approach to chemotherapy is polymer wafer implants. In this approach, wafers made of a biodegradable material are saturated with a chemotherapy drug. Then, when a tumor is removed, the wafers are inserted into the hole. They slowly dissolve, delivering the chemo-therapy agent directly to the tumor site to kill any remaining cancer cells. An advantage of this approach is that it can be used to deliver a higher dose of chemotherapy medication than is possible with conventional intravenous or oral approaches because there is less need to worry about the effect on normal cells elsewhere in the body.

Research is also being undertaken to find medications that patients can take to protect themselves from the side effects of chemotherapy. Specific drugs are being developed to protect organs such as the heart, kidneys, and bladder.

BETTER RADIATION THERAPY

Researchers are attempting to develop a new type of drug that would make radiation therapy more effective. This type of drug is called a radiosensitizer because it makes cancer cells more sensitive to radiation. However, this work is still in the early phases. It is unclear yet whether radiosensitizers currently under investigation, such as misonidazole and metronidazole, will have the desired effect of making tumors more vulnerable to radiation.

TREATING TUMORS WITH HEAT

Tumors are sensitive to heat because they lack the well-developed set of blood vessels that normal tissues have to cool them. Some researchers are testing a variety of approaches to heating tumors in the hope of killing the cancer cells. Scientists implant tiny antennas in the tumors and then try to transmit heat energy to them through the antennas. Experiments are being conducted using microwaves, sound waves, and electromagnetic waves. It is not yet known, however, whether this approach will be effective.

NEW GENES

Gene therapy is another area being explored to treat brain cancer. Gene therapy relies on the infusion into the patient's bloodstream of deactivated virus cells into which a gene designed for a specific purpose has been inserted. The virus particles enter the cancer cells and insert the gene they carry into the cancer cell's DNA. When the cancer cell reproduces, the new cells incorporate the implanted DNA. This new DNA either inhibits the expression of the cancer-causing gene, replaces the defective gene with a healthy gene, or initiates the production of a compound that causes the defective cell to behave in an appropriate (noncancerous) way. Before this method can be widely adopted, however, scientists must establish not only that the new gene will be effective but also that introducing the new gene will not have unexpected consequences.

IMMUNOTHERAPY

Immunotherapy is aimed at using the patient's own immune system to kill cancer cells. In one approach, the patient is given a stimulant,

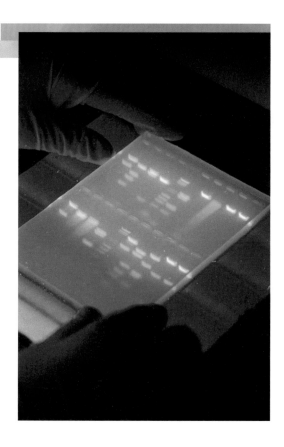

A researcher uses a technique called gel electrophoresis to sort and analyze DNA strands in an attempt to identify genetic mutations that may increase the risk for certain types of disease.

such as interleukin-2, which is designed to enhance the patient's immune system activity. The idea is that the patient's own immune system cells will find and kill cancer cells. If the immune system's activity can be increased, then more cancer cells will be killed. Exactly how effective this type of approach will be is not yet clear.

Another immunotherapy approach that is being studied uses lab-grown antibodies attached to a toxin to kill cancer cells. A type of antibody called monoclonal antibodies is grown in a lab. "Monoclonal" means that the antibodies are all identical. Scientists grow a type of antibody that will attach itself to cancer cells. Then, they attach a toxic substance to these antibodies and inject them into the patient's body. The antibodies attach to the tumor, inserting the toxin into the cancer cells, killing them. This approach has shown some promise in treating

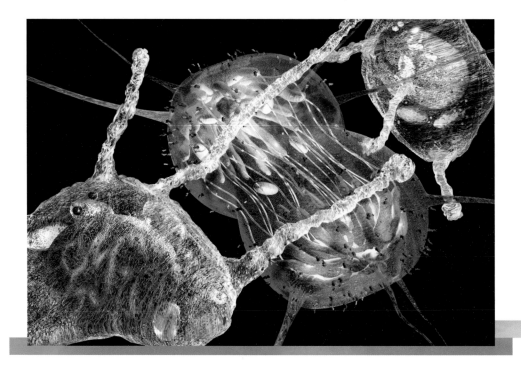

Here, macrophages (white blood cells that attack other cells), in response to the injection of a cancer vaccine, identify, surround, and attack a cancer cell (center) while it attempts to divide and replicate.

certain types of cancer, but it is not yet clear whether this approach will be successful in treating solid tumors such as those commonly found in brain cancer.

Researchers are very interested in the possibilities the immune system presents for using the body's own defenses against cancer. These cutting-edge studies, together with the work currently being done in the areas of chemotherapy, radiation therapy, and gene therapy, may help defeat one of humanity's most dreaded diseases. Someday soon, this research may lead to a medical breakthrough that will help dramatically swell the ranks of people who have not only survived brain cancer but are also thriving many years after successful treatment.

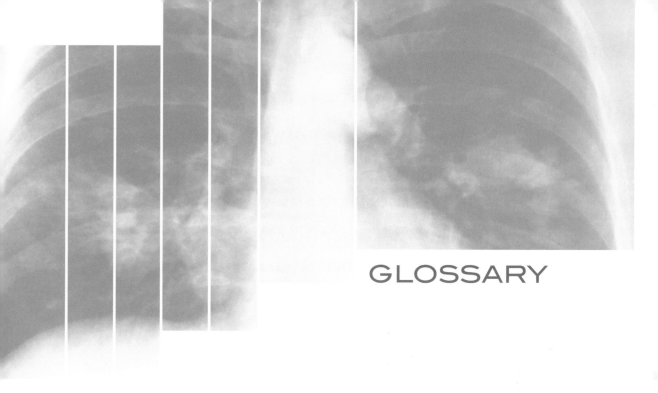

GLOSSARY

benign tumor A slow-growing tumor that is unlikely to metastasize, or spread elsewhere.

cerebellum The part of the brain above and behind the brain stem, at the back of the head.

convulsions Involuntary contractions of the muscles that cause the body to shake violently.

craniotomy A surgical procedure in which the skull is opened.

gene A tiny sequence of genetic material that controls the production of specific proteins that regulate certain body functions.

glial tumor A tumor that grows from the cells of the fibers that support the nerve cells in the brain.

malignant tumor A fast-growing, aggressive form of cancer.

metastasize To spread.

myelin A fatty material that sheaths and protects the nerve cells of the brain.

neurologist A doctor who specializes in treating diseases of the brain and spinal cord.

nonglial tumor A tumor that grows from the cells of nerves, glands, or blood vessels in the brain.

occupational therapist An expert who assists people with disabilities in developing techniques to meet the demands of daily living and work.

oncologist A doctor who specializes in treating cancer.

pituitary gland A gland in the brain that releases hormones that regulate growth, among other things.

tumor A mass of cells that is reproducing and growing out of control.

FOR MORE INFORMATION

American Brain Tumor Association
2720 River Road
Des Plaines, IL 60018
(800) 886-2282
Web site: http://www.abta.org
The American Brain Tumor Association is a not-for-profit, independent
    organization. It seeks to eliminate brain tumors through research
    and meet the needs of brain tumor patients and their families.

American Cancer Society
National Home Office
250 Williams Street NW
Atlanta, GA 30303-1002
(800) 227-2345
Web site: http://www.cancer.org
The American Cancer Society is a nationwide, community-based,
    voluntary health organization dedicated to eliminating cancer as
    a major health problem by preventing cancer, saving lives, and

diminishing suffering from cancer through research, education, advocacy, and service.

Brain Tumor Society
124 Watertown Street, Suite 3H
Watertown, MA 02472
(800) 770-8287, ext. 25
Web site: http://www.tbts.org
The Brain Tumor Society exists to find a cure for brain tumors and improve the quality of life of brain tumor patients, survivors, and their families by providing access to psychosocial support, information, and resources.

Centers for Disease Control and Prevention (CDC)
1600 Clifton Road
Atlanta, GA 30333
(404) 639-3311
Web site: http://www.cdc.gov
The CDC is one operating component of the Department of Health and Human Services, the principal agency in the U.S. government that protects the health and safety of all Americans. The CDC is at the forefront of public health efforts to prevent and control infectious and chronic diseases, injuries, workplace hazards, disabilities, and environmental health threats.

Children's Brain Tumor Foundation
274 Madison Avenue, Suite 1004
New York, NY 10016
(212) 448-9494
(866) CBT-HOPE (228-4673)
Web site: http://www.cbtf.org

The Children's Brain Tumor Foundation, a nonprofit organization, was founded in 1988 by dedicated parents, physicians, and friends. Its mission is to improve the treatment, quality of life, and long-term outlook for children with brain and spinal cord tumors through research, support, education, and advocacy.

Mayo Clinic
200 First Street SW
Rochester, MN 55905
(507) 284-2511
Web site: http://www.mayoclinic.org
Mayo Clinic is a not-for-profit medical practice dedicated to the diagnosis and treatment of virtually every type of complex illness. Its staff members, including doctors, specialists, and other health care professionals, provide comprehensive diagnosis, understandable answers, and effective treatment.

National Cancer Institute (NCI)
National Institutes of Health, DHHS
6116 Executive Boulevard, Suite 3036A, MSC 8322
Bethesda, MD 20892-8322
(800) 4-CANCER (422-6237)
Web site: http://www.cancer.gov
The NCI is a component of the National Institutes of Health and is the U.S. government's principal agency for cancer research and training. It coordinates the National Cancer Program, which conducts and supports research, training, health information dissemination, and other programs with respect to the cause, diagnosis, prevention, and treatment of cancer, rehabilitation from cancer, and the continuing care of cancer patients and the families of cancer patients.

National Institute of Neurological Disorders and Stroke (NINDS)
Brain Resources and Information Network (BRAIN)
P.O. Box 5801
Bethesda, MD 20824
(800) 352-9424
Web site: http://www.ninds.nih.gov
The mission of NINDS is to reduce the burden of neurological disease
   mainly by conducting, fostering, coordinating, and guiding research
   on the causes, prevention, diagnosis, and treatment of neurological
   disorders and stroke, and the supporting of basic research in related
   scientific areas.

National Organization for Rare Disorders (NORD)
P.O. Box 1968
55 Kenosia Avenue
Danbury, CT 06813-1968
(203) 744-0100
Web site: http://www.rarediseases.org
NORD is a federation of voluntary health organizations dedicated
   to helping people with rare diseases and assisting the organizations
   that serve them. It is committed to the identification, treatment, and
   cure of rare disorders through education, advocacy, research,
   and service.

WEB SITES

Due to the changing nature of Internet links, Rosen Publishing has
developed an online list of Web sites related to the subject of this book.
This site is updated regularly. Please use this link to access the list:

http://www.rosenlinks.com/cms/brai

FOR FURTHER READING

Black, Peter McLaren. *Living with a Brain Tumor: Dr. Peter Black's Guide to Taking Control of Your Treatment.* New York, NY: Owl Books, 2006.

Caldwell, Wilma A. *Cancer Information for Teens: Health Tips About Cancer Awareness, Prevention, Diagnosis, and Treatment.* Detroit, MI: Omnigraphics, 2004.

Clark, Arda Darakjian. *Diseases and Disorders: Brain Tumors.* San Diego, CA: Lucent Books, 2006.

Feuerstein, Michael, and Patricia Findley. *The Cancer Survivor's Guide: The Essential Handbook to Life After Cancer.* New York, NY: Marlowe & Co., 2006.

Harpham, Wendy Schlessel. *Happiness in a Storm: Facing Illness and Embracing Life as a Healthy Survivor.* New York, NY: W. W. Norton, 2005.

Karren, Keith J., et al. *Mind/Body Health: The Effects of Attitudes, Emotions, and Relationships.* Upper Saddle River, NJ: Benjamin Cummings, 2005.

Katz, Bob. *Elaine's Circle: A Teacher, a Student, a Classroom, and One Unforgettable Year.* New York, NY: Avalon, 2005.

Keane, Maureen, and Daniella Chace. *What to Eat If You Have Cancer.* New York, NY: McGraw-Hill, 2006.

Mareck, Amy. *Fighting for My Life: Growing up with Cancer.* Minneapolis, MN: Fairview Press, 2007.

Silverstein, Alvin, et al. *Cancer: Conquering a Deadly Disease.* Minneapolis, MN: Twenty-First Century Books, 2004.

Stark-Vance, Virginia, and M. L. Dubay. *100 Questions and Answers About Brain Tumors.* Boston, MA: Jones & Bartlett, 2003.

Wyborny, Sheila. *Science on the Edge: Cancer Treatments.* Farmington Hills, MI: Blackbirch Press, 2005.

Zeltzer, Paul M. *Brain Tumors: Leaving the Garden of Eden: A Survival Guide to Diagnosis, Learning the Basics, Getting Organized, and Finding Your Medical Team.* San Diego, CA: Lucent Books, 2006.

American Brain Tumor Association. "A Primer of Brain Tumors." 2007. Retrieved May 2008 (http://www.abta.org/index.cfm?contentid=170).

American Cancer Society. "Detailed Guide: Brain/CNS Tumors in Adults." Retrieved May 2008 (http://www.cancer.org/docroot/CRI/CRI_2_3x.asp?rnav=cridg&dt=3).

American Cancer Society. "What Are the Risk Factors for Brain and Spinal Cord Tumors in Adults?" 2006. Retrieved May 2008 (http://www.cancer.org/docroot/cri/content/cri_2_4_2x_what_are_the_risk_factors_for_brain_and_spinal_cord_tumors_3.asp?sitearea=cri).

Baehring, Joachim M., and Joseph M. Piepmeier, eds. *Brain Tumors: Practical Guide to Diagnosis and Treatment*. New York, NY: Informa Healthcare USA, 2006.

Brain Tumor Society. "Common Brain Tumors." Retrieved May 2008 (http://www.tbts.org/itemDetail.asp?categoryID=292&itemID=16532).

Brain Tumor Society. "Treatment Options." Retrieved May 2008 (http://www.tbts.org/itemDetail.asp?categoryID=368&itemID=16380).

Brain Tumor Society. "What to Expect After Neurosurgery." Retrieved May 2008 (http://www.tbts.org/assets/files/Fact%20Sheets/After_ Neurosurgery.pdf).

DeMonte, Franco, et al., eds. *Tumors of the Brain and Spine* (M.D. Anderson Cancer Care Series). New York, NY: Springer Science + Business Media, LLC, 2007.

MedlinePlus. "Brain Cancer." Retrieved May 2008 (http://www.nlm.nih. gov/medlineplus/braincancer.html).

Meeks, Linda, and Philip Heit. *Health and Wellness*. New York, NY: McGrawHill/Glencoe, 2005.

National Brain Tumor Foundation. "The Essential Guide to Brain Tumors." 2007. Retrieved May 2008 (http://www.braintumor.org/upload/ contents/330/GuideFINAL2007.pdf).

National Cancer Institute. "Adult Brain Tumors Treatment." Retrieved May 2008 (http://www.cancer.gov/cancertopics/pdq/treatment/ adultbrain/patient/).

National Institute of Neurological Disorders and Stroke. "NINDS Brain and Spinal Tumors Information Page." Retrieved May 2008 (http://www.ninds.nih.gov/disorders/brainandspinaltumors/ brainandspinaltumors.htm).

Newton, Herbert B., ed. *Handbook of Brain Tumor Chemotherapy*. Burlington, MA: Academic Press, 2005.

Padilla, Michael J., et al. *Human Biology and Health*. Upper Saddle River, NJ: Pearson, 2004.

Panno, Joseph, Ph.D. *Cancer: The Role of Genes, Lifestyle, and Environment*. New York, NY: Facts On File, 2004.

RadiologyInfo. "Computed Tomography (CT)—Head." 2007. Retrieved May 2008 (http://www.radiologyinfo.org/en/info.cfm?pg= headct&bhcp=1).

RadiologyInfo. "Functional MR Imaging (fMRI)—Brain." 2007. Retrieved May 2008 (http://www.radiologyinfo.org/en/info.cfm?pg=fmribrain).

RadiologyInfo. "MRI of the Head." 2007. Retrieved May 2008 (http://www.radiologyinfo.org/en/info.cfm?pg=headmr).

Raizer, Jeffrey J., and Lauren E. Abrey, eds. *Brain Metastases* (Cancer Treatment and Research). New York, NY: Springer Science + Business Media, LLC, 2007.

Shiminski-Maher, Tania. *Childhood Brain and Spinal Cord Tumors: A Guide for Families, Friends, and Caregivers.* Sebastopol, CA: Patient Centered Guides, 2001.

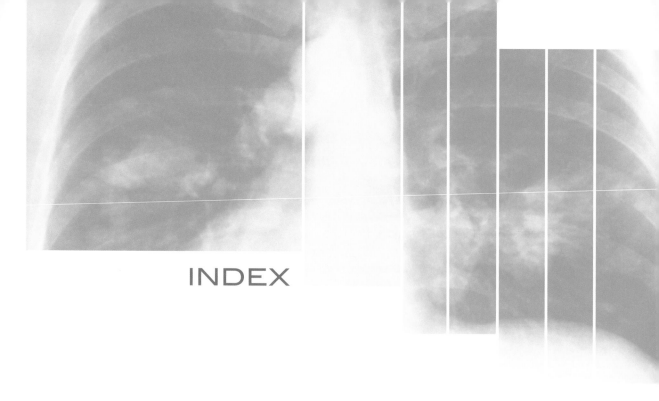

INDEX

ABOUT THE AUTHOR

Jeri Freedman earned a B.A. degree from Harvard University. For fifteen years, she worked for companies in the medical field. Among the numerous books she has written for young adults are *The Human Population and the Nitrogen Cycle*, *Hemophilia*, *Hepatitis B*, *Lymphoma: Current and Emerging Trends in Detection and Treatment*, *How Do We Know About Genetics and Heredity?*, *The Mental and Physical Effects of Obesity*, *Autism*, *Tay-Sachs Disease*, and *Applications and Limitations of Taxonomy in Classification of Organisms: An Anthology of Current Thought*.

PHOTO CREDITS

Cover, p. 1 © Pasieka/Photo Researchers; cover (corner photo), pp. 4, 5 © Punchstock; back cover and throughout, pp. 11, 24, 25, 32, 33, 43 © National Cancer Institute; p. 5 (top) Courtesy of Cassidy and Pinkard Colliers; p. 8 © Nucleus MedicalArt/Visuals Unlimited; pp. 10, 13 © Claus Lunau/Bonnier Publications/Photo Researchers; p. 14 © Dr. Kessell and Dr. Kardon/Tissues and Organs/Visuals Unlimited; p. 21 © www.istockphoto.com/Dragana Djorovic; p. 23 © Will and Deni McIntyre/Photo Researchers; p. 30 © Phanie/Photo Researchers; p. 35 © Getty Images; p. 36 © www.istockphoto.com/Claudia Dewald; p. 38 © www.istockphoto.com/Lisa F. Young; p. 40 © Richard T. Nowitz/Phototake; p. 42 © www.istockphoto.com/Angel Rodriguez; p. 46 © David McCarthy/Photo Researchers; p. 49 © LookatSciences/Phototake; p. 50 © XVIVO LLC/Phototake.

Designer: Evelyn Horovicz; Photo Researcher: Marty Levick